SAN FRANCISCO Scavenger

Jill K. Robinson

REEDY PRESS

Reedy Press
PO Box 5131
St. Louis, MO 63139, USA
www.reedypress.com

Library of Congress Control Number: 2023938886

ISBN: 9781681064871

Cover and interior design by Claire Ford

Cover and interior photos by the author unless otherwise noted.

Clip art courtesy of Pixabay and Wikimedia Commons

Printed in the United States of America
23 24 25 26 27 5 4 3 2 1

Dedication

To the city of San Francisco
and all who fall in love with her.

Contents

Acknowledgments

Thank you to my family and friends who suggested their favorite classic and quirky San Francisco landmarks for this book. Our many adventures in the City by the Bay will always be among my best memories.

And to San Francisco, my beloved, magical city, you have always held my heart.

Introduction

After the Ohlone peoples had lived in the region for thousands of years, many of San Francisco's early visitors came in search of gold and silver treasure. Ever since, people have sought a wide variety of different kinds of treasure: fame, wealth, property, inspiration, love, family, community, freedom, and a fresh start. Some have stayed, others have left their hearts.

As a Bay Area child, my first big city was San Francisco. On a regular basis, I felt that a certain kind of magic lived here, and all I had to do was turn the right corner. The feeling hasn't left me. A good part of the fun I had in writing this book (as well as *100 Things to Do in San Francisco Before You Die, Second Edition,* which I co-authored with Kimberley Lovato) was to revisit many of the places I grew up getting to know and love—and even learn something new about them.

Whether it's an old classic or a newer addition to San Francisco, all these sites had something to teach me. If you have even the faintest glimmer of an adventurous spirit, I hope you let them teach you, too. Perhaps you chose this book because you love the thrill of solving a puzzle, or have a desire to learn a little history. Maybe it's the urge to get out and explore, or even rediscover a city you thought you knew. San Francisco is worth getting to know on a deeper level.

This book features 19 different neighborhoods across the 49 square miles of San Francisco, each with eight to 32 sites that you can see for yourself. As you wander through these neighborhoods and find things that interest you, I hope you investigate further, and become acquainted with the true spirit of San Francisco.

Legend

1 Castro

2 Chinatown

3 Civic Center

4 Downtown

5 Embarcadero/ Fisherman's Wharf

6 Financial District

7 Golden Gate Park

8 Haight-Ashbury

9 Japantown/ Western Addition

10 Marina

11 Mission

12 Nob Hill

13 North Beach/ Telegraph Hill

14 Pacific Heights

15 Presidio

16 Richmond/Lincoln Park

17 Russian Hill

18 SoMa/South Beach

19 Sunset

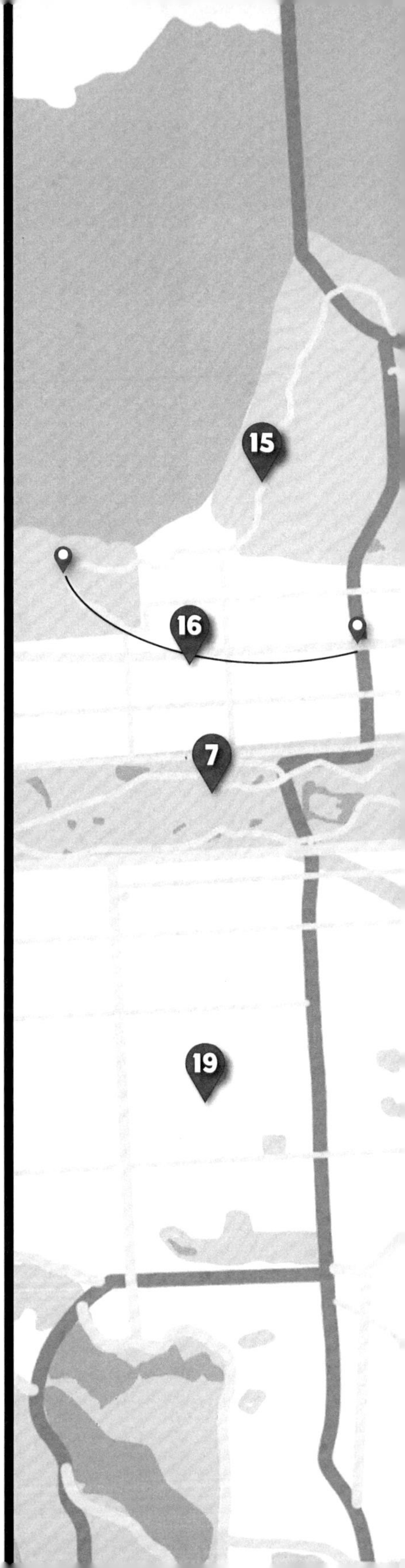

5
10
13
17
2
6
14
12
18
9
4
3
8
11
1

Castro

Both historic and youthful, the Castro district is San Francisco's enduring LGBTQIA+ haven. Beloved for its rainbows, welcoming spirit, small businesses, low-key watering holes, and joyful nightclubs, this neighborhood is where you can be your authentic self.

1

Even more than 100 years,
This building has been filled with cheers.
Frequent visitor or newbie,
You'll thrill when you see the marquee.

2

When you walk along Castro Street,
Don't miss this tribute at your feet.
Honors the work of pioneers,
Positive impact through the years.

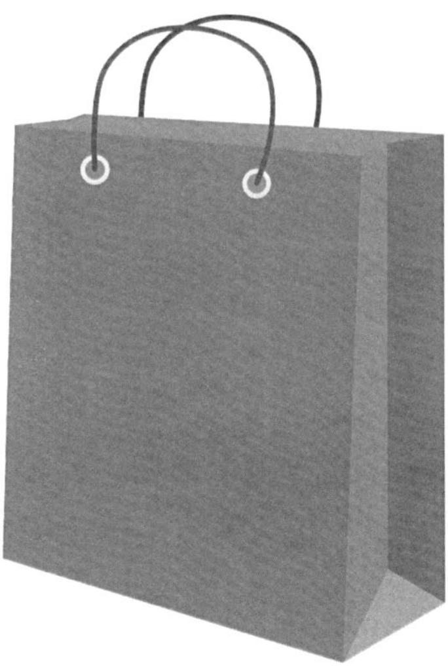

3

Needing home goods or souvenirs?
You'll sure score big if you stop here.
Clever minds designed the front window;
Stop to admire the tableau.

4

This landmark, a very important link
To remember those with the color pink.
Once a symbol of punishment and shame;
Now, pride and resilience it does proclaim.

5

A former shop for a visual art
Marks a special place in the Castro's heart.
It doubled as a campaign headquarters
For a beloved man and his supporters.

6

With a mission of acceptance and pride,
For history, this place is your guide.
First of its kind in the United States,
Behind its doors, understanding awaits.

____

____

7

When Castro residents take to the street,
Fabulous clothes never take a back seat.
This artful acknowledgment of protest
At a place named after an epic quest.

____

____

8

A world where un-judged love awaits
Is what this item celebrates.
It includes a familiar sight,
Painted with a color that's bright.

9

When you are craving something sweet,
This is the place to get a treat.
It's hard to choose a favorite,
But when you do, just savor it.

10

While it's not the yellow brick road,
Perfect placement at this crossroad.
Corners connected by rainbows:
Better to see when traffic slows.

11

It almost feels like you're a spy,
Windows to watch the world go by.
Here at the neighborhood's gateway
For refreshment at a mainstay.

12

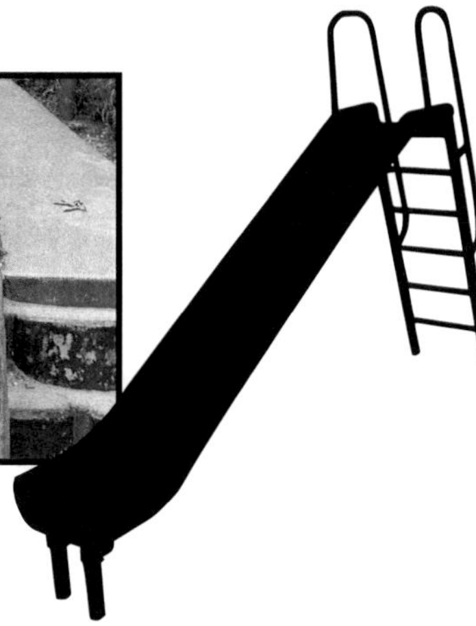

Put down this book, close the pages,
Enjoy this spot for all ages.
Let kids go first to earn goodwill,
Then it's your turn to go downhill.

13

Luring fans of science, nature, and art,
Note a local woman gave it a start.
As a part of its continued mission,
When you walk inside, there's no admission.

14

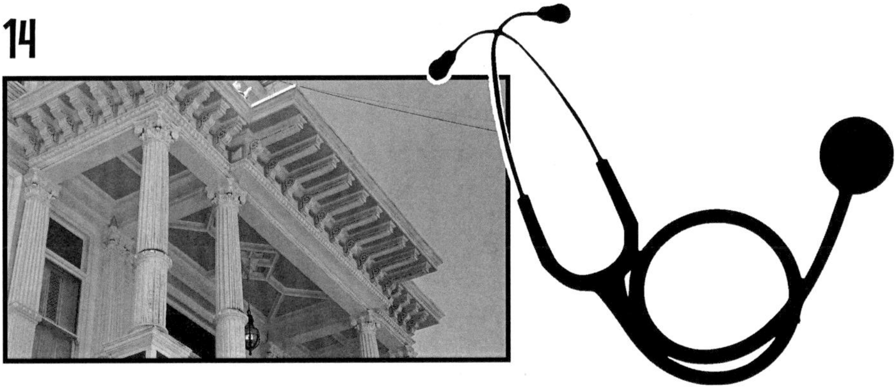

Known for its baroque, Queen Anne style,
A building that will make you smile.
Built by a man with shady wealth,
Once used as a center for health.

15

Through the neighborhood, as you roam,
Look for a golden onion dome.
Queen Anne architecture you see
Untouched by quake: not one degree.

Chinatown

North America's first and largest Chinatown is right here in San Francisco, but when you're in this bustling neighborhood, it's easy to think that you're far, far away. The streets flood the senses, and much of the same cultural architecture still remains from its 19th-century days.

1

Made from brick brought around Cape Horn,
This building of red brick was born.
Its tower, a clock face on each side,
Showing from time, you cannot hide.

2

Facing south, these three street portals
Are not for gods, but for mortals.
Nod to the lions as you go
To tell these guards you're not a foe.

3

This simple spot is off the charts
For those who love egg custard tarts.
When it's open, it is a sign
You'll taste one soon: just get in line.

4

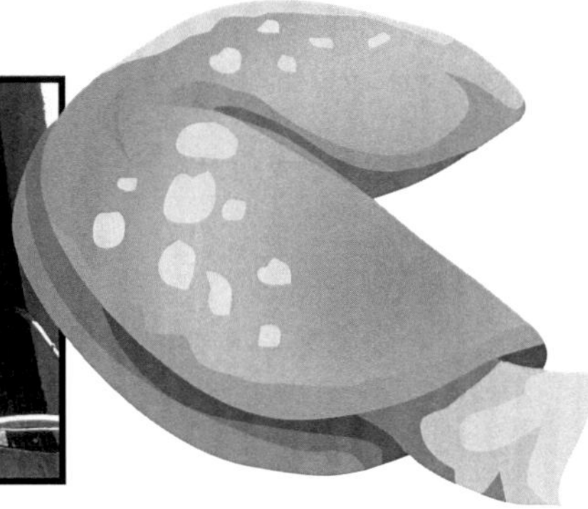

Senses take over, just follow your nose:
Sweet smell in the air, just watch your pace slow.
Daily production is in numbers great,
Crack just one open and you'll learn your fate.

5

Here, in the place where this city began,
Look well for this remembrance of a man.
You may know him for his well-told stories;
He lived here at the start of his glories.

6

A search for cuisine Cantonese
Will find you here, not overseas.
Place your order, no need to grab.
Best-known dish? Salt-and-pepper crab.

7

The water can flow; the water can crash,
Become what it's poured into, with a splash.
Find this tribute to the king of kung fu
And see if you can be like water, too.

8

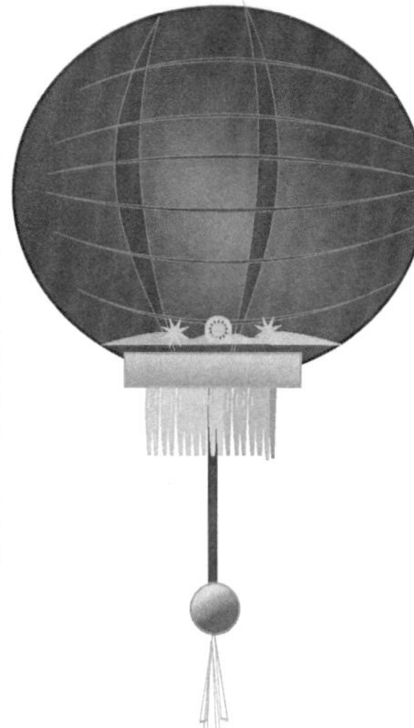

Named for the goddess of the sea,
This temple on floor number three.
With lanterns the color of flame,
It's known by its Cantonese name.

9

Founded when we became a state,
This temple has served numbers great.
Hoping her husband wouldn't lose,
Bess Truman sought election news.

10

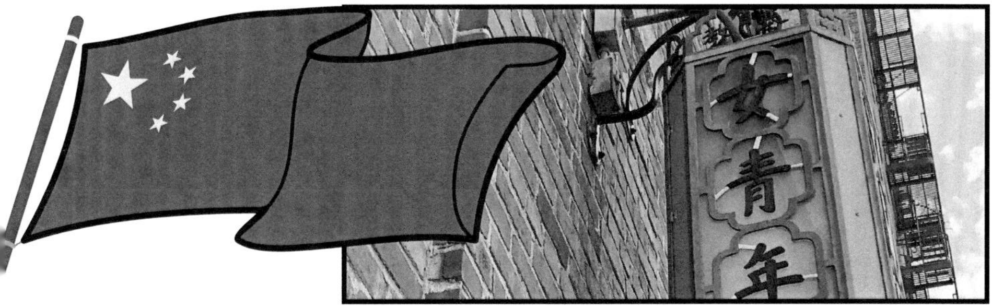

Designed by a famed local architect,
This building is a place of great respect.
Insight into Asian community,
Skipping is a missed opportunity.

11

Founded more than 100 years ago,
A following continues to grow.
Subject of writers, and even greater,
Was once home to "the world's rudest waiter."

12

A tranquil spot away from commotion,
A president from across the ocean.
Sculptor and subject had earlier met,
Making this art special from the outset.

13

For great cuisine, there's no need to go far:
Visit this place with a Michelin star.
Its locally-born chef has also scored
The very prestigious James Beard award.

14

This building, a longtime shelter for books,
Has kept its Italian Renaissance looks.
Built thanks to funds from a rich steel tycoon,
For San Franciscans, this place was a boon.

15

This commemorative marker is the site
Of a place that brought academic light.
The former structure, built by volunteers,
For the children of the early pioneers.

16

With more than 13,000 calls a day,
This site's operators could never play.
Great experts in language and dialect,
They always made important calls connect.

17

The oldest of its kind in Chinatown,
This business operates with great renown.
If you are in search of tasty mooncakes,
A visit is like winning the sweepstakes.

18

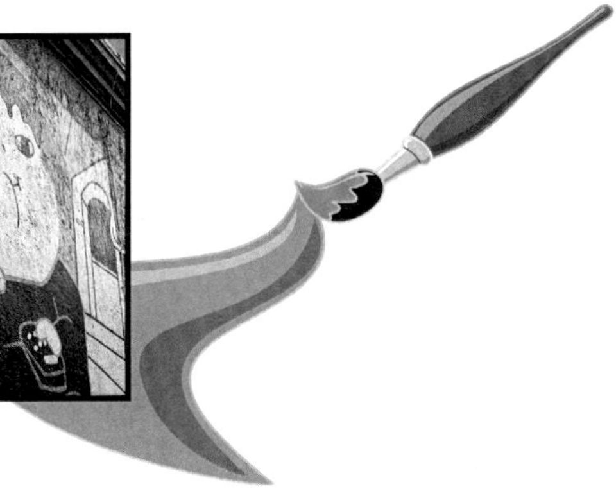

By two women it was painted,
Two generations, acquainted.
Quirky images and folk art;
Experience speaks to the heart.

19

If you are craving a savory treat,
Look for an alley, don't look for a street.
Opened 1920, this would become
The first in the US to serve dim sum.

Civic Center

The optimistic "City Beautiful" movement of the early 20th century inspired the Beaux-Arts-style buildings in San Francisco's Civic Center. Home to city infrastructure and many of San Francisco's performing arts organizations, the neighborhood also has a wealth of restaurants.

307 FEET

1

Beaux-Arts building with a majestic dome,
Taller than the nation's capitol home.
The building's architect made no mistake
Replacing the first, victim of the quake.

2

Built during the Great Depression,
Site for artistic expression.
Funded by local donation,
Honors those who served their nation.

3

It would seem this building is quite content
Showcasing items from one continent.
Central place of cultural connection,
For locals, it inspires affection.

4

From a great global exposition,
For events, it has held great tradition.
Named after a rock impresario,
Go here to enjoy a memorable show.

5

Ivory building with curvy glass
Is known for music that's world-class.
Its architects used a few tricks
To give it top-notch acoustics.

6

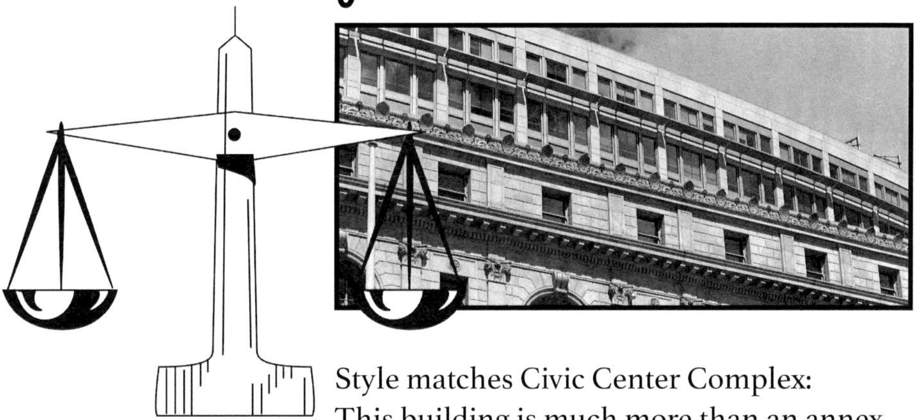

Style matches Civic Center Complex:
This building is much more than an annex.
It's home to a court that is most supreme
And named for a man held in high esteem.

7

This structure, built for elaborate show,
Is located on the old Auto Row.
At the entrance, look up as you stand back
To see the frieze honoring Cadillac.

8

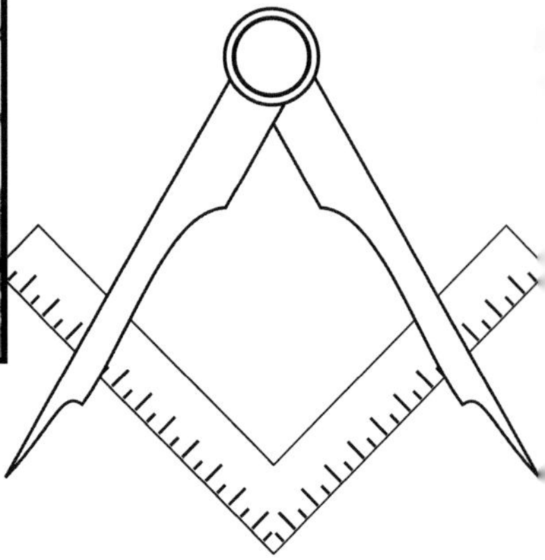

Once a temple for great ceremony,
Home to a secretive patrimony.
Façade carvings are a beautiful thing:
Look for the one with a biblical king.

9

A building with ornate Plateresque style,
Façade with an elaborate profile.
Home to great entertainment of the stage,
Productions tell stories of every age.

10

This building is not yet 30 years old:
Its important treasure greater than gold.
The hub of many, this one is called "Main,"
With wealth inside, the outside is not plain.

11

Blanco's, in the Barbary Coast era,
Was well-known as far as the Sierra.
Entertainment evolved over the years,
Today, providing music for your ears.

12

During your tour of the fine arts district,
Don't miss this building with its statistic.
The first stand-alone structure of its kind,
Built only for jazz, it has been defined.

13

This spacious church made of red brick
Survived the earthquake: quite a trick.
Dodging resulting fires bright,
Near structures blown by dynamite.

14

This is the lone and final resting place
For one who sought equality of race.
Long a champion of Yosemite:
For its protection, ever he did plea.

15

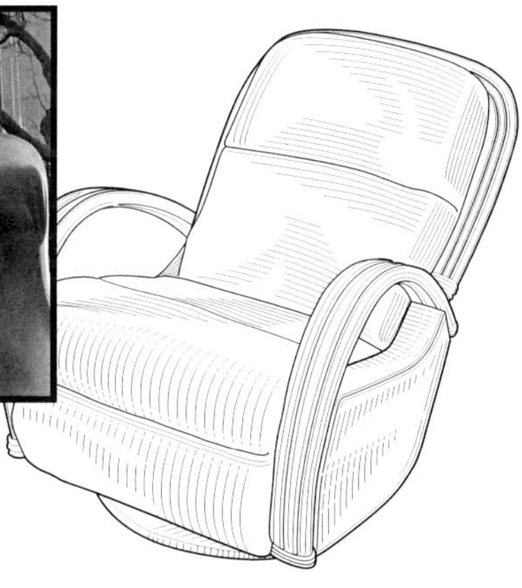

Near a building known for its curves,
Reclining figure soothes the nerves.
Bronze sculpture by an English man
Adds beauty to the civic plan.

Downtown

With the city's finest department stores, the theater district, and gritty city life, San Francisco's downtown area combines everything one might expect in a large metropolitan area. While shopping is a major draw here, historical gems shine right in plain sight.

1

Soaring building of art deco,
Maya designs, it does echo.
Décor on all 26 floors,
You enter through gold-colored doors.

2

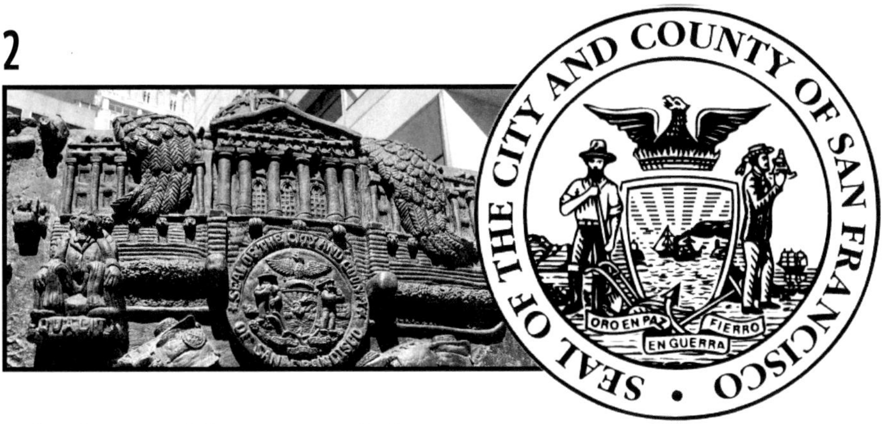

A landscape of the city, cast in bronze,
Includes beloved landmarks and icons.
Meticulous study it does entail;
It's easy to get lost in the detail.

3

This flatiron, in glazed terra-cotta,
Has the creamy color of ricotta.
Sadly the first was burned in a fire,
This second version we can admire.

4

High atop a column sits this statue
Of Nike (the goddess, but not the shoe).
It's dedicated to a war hero:
The chances that you'll miss it are zero.

5

Well-used by Bernhardt and Duncan,
This place's fame has not shrunk(en).
With different names through the years,
The interior echoes with cheers.

6

Named for a man schooled in the arts,
Music and business were his smarts.
With Shubert formed a partnership,
Making this a West Coast flagship.

7

It opened as a vaudeville house,
This building larger than a mouse.
Hosting performers its whole life,
With quality shows, it is rife.

8

The rich estate of one of the Big Four
Funded this grand building from the ground floor.
Look up high for a glass elevator:
For moving views, few places are greater.

9

Unassuming exterior
Hides a bar that's superior.
Warm and cozy Parisian style
Makes happy-hour patrons smile.

10

A temple in its early years,
Like other buildings, changed careers.
True Arabian-esque design,
Called a home to acting quite fine.

11

First of its kind, post-earthquake and fire,
Beaux-Arts design for all to admire.
With a doorway arch and columns noble,
Such beauty for a job that's so mobile.

12

Perched on the street like the prow of a ship,
This building's history is not a blip.
Former office to a friend of Sam Spade,
Its sandstone façade, for years, has long stayed.

13

Among the bustle, this place to relax
Is sunken down near the turntable tracks.
Named for a local railway inventor,
Look for his monument in this center.

14

Please look carefully for this simple sight,
Only SF place by a man named Wright.
The exterior certainly striking;
The inside is what has tourists spiking.

15

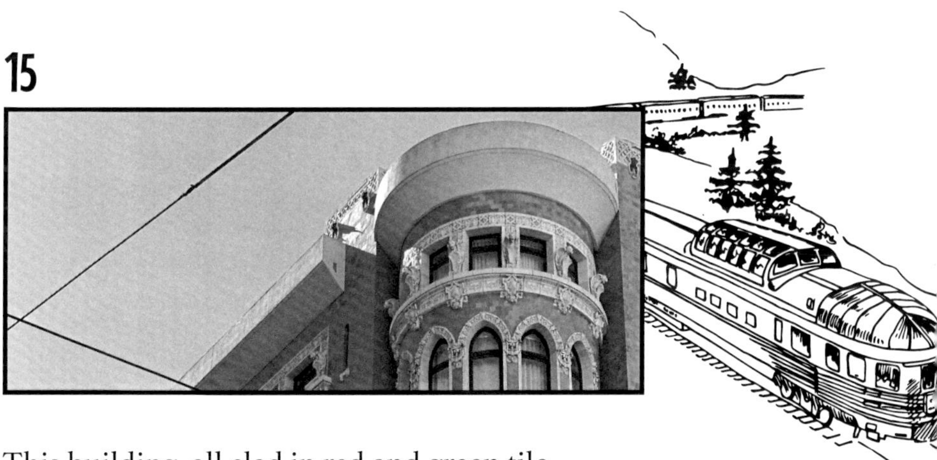

This building, all clad in red and green tile,
Stands out from others with its unique style.
Built by a former railway architect
Whose work in concrete we do now protect.

16

Is this the Roman Pantheon?
Strong, yet elegant: like a swan.
A solid structure, like big tank,
Its initial purpose, a bank.

17

From day one, headlines it did make,
Building named for explorer Drake.
Although it sports a different name,
Its history remains the same.

18

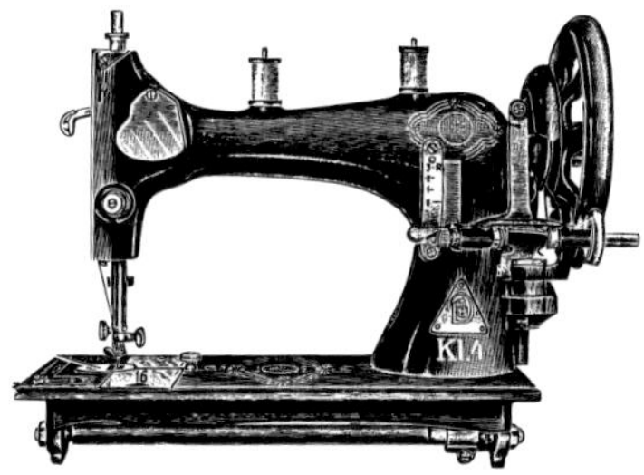

A landmark here since '52,
Serving customers old and new.
Haven for fine inspiration,
Lures fans from around the nation.

19

This venue, built for vaudeville shows,
The artists through the years were pros.
Chaplin to Dylan, and the Dead,
A stage where famous feet have tread.

20

Here, love and acceptance abide:
As you approach, be sure to glide.
Social justice among its goals,
This kind community of souls.

21

To serve immigrants, this church was founded,
Near a French quarter it became grounded.
Rebuilt after the great fire and earthquake,
Its soaring presence is not a mistake.

22

Time flees swiftly on the sidewalk,
Nearby traffic in a gridlock.
Commissioned by a watchmaker,
Marker of time, not a taker.

23

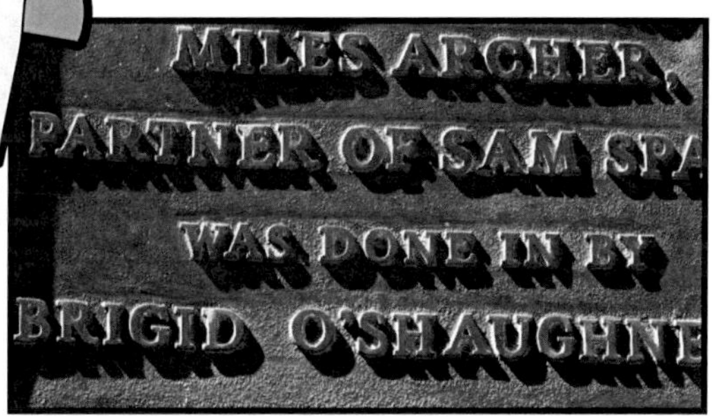

Are these people real or fiction?
Story has caused some addiction.
Obsessive greed in her pursuit
Caused her death, chasing after loot.

Embarcadero/ Fisherman's Wharf

While San Francisco's waterfront has evolved from its days as a gold rush hub, immigration center, and fishing capital, much of that energy still can be felt here—along the wide Embarcadero that sweeps from Market Street up to Fisherman's Wharf.

1

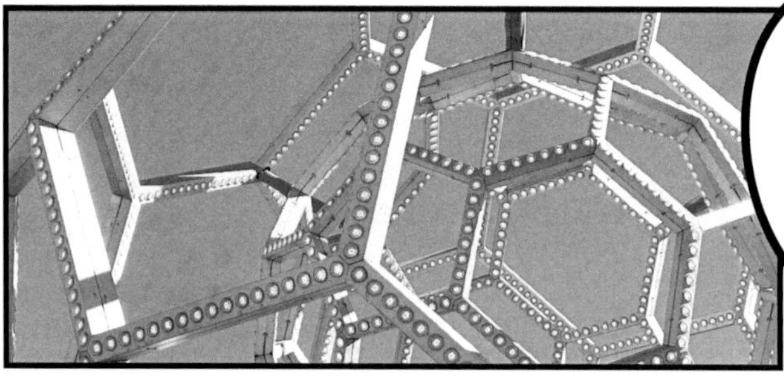

This hands-on center of art and science
Has a nontraditional alliance.
By making science something you can see,
Learning and understanding grows: that's key.

2

This stark and connected concrete tangle
Was next to the freeway, at an angle.
Freeway's gone, but opinions are expressed
At this spot that's a magnet for protest.

3

A welcome sight to those on ships,
This building marked the end of trips.
Dramatic tower is a sight
From land or water, day or night.

4

This tribute to nonviolent resistance
In all weather, maintains its persistence.
In bronze, the icon stands for the masses;
Thieves have been known to steal its eyeglasses.

5

Easygoing and relaxed, like blue jeans,
This urban space, best enjoyed without screens.
Home to a company known for work pants,
The garden is a welcome place for plants.

6

They're problematic in a shake,
But bricks were still used post-earthquake.
A warehouse, close to piers and train,
Is one of the few that remain.

7

Gold Rush-era ship was driven aground,
Not seaworthy, it was perfectly sound.
Used as a bar until it was landlocked,
Beneath your feet, it's permanently docked.

8

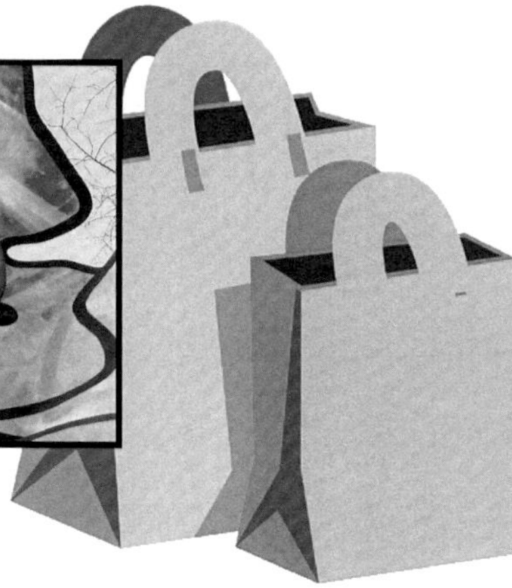

These curved pieces of stainless steel,
To some, they have a great appeal.
Too large to fit in shopping bags,
Depicting a woman dressed in rags.

9

In old days, once upon a time,
There was a railroad: the Beltline.
On the waterfront, a great fit,
This roundhouse is what's left of it.

10

Along the waterfront, if you're wishing
To enjoy the outdoors and go fishing,
This pier is a great place to cast your line,
And the view from here is really quite fine.

11

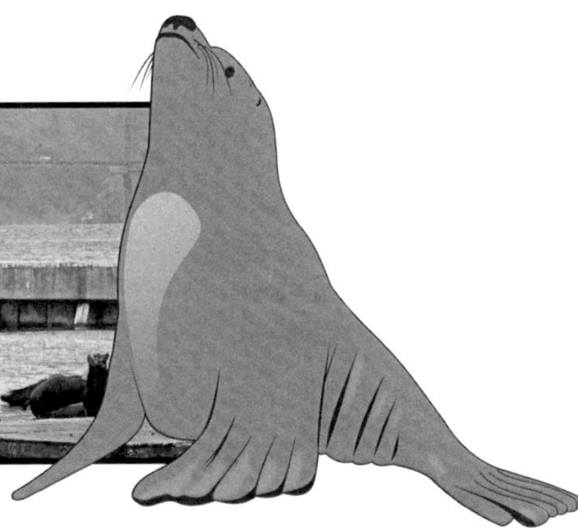

Sometimes they're here, sometimes they're not;
You'll know if you're within earshot.
This haulout is for warmth and rest;
Together, they're one big bark fest.

12

With more than 300 machines,
It figures in a gamer's dreams.
Open every day of the year,
Beloved arcade machines are here.

13

Someone's love for San Francisco
Inspired this organ aglow.
Open your heart to find this love
Right in front of you, not above.

14

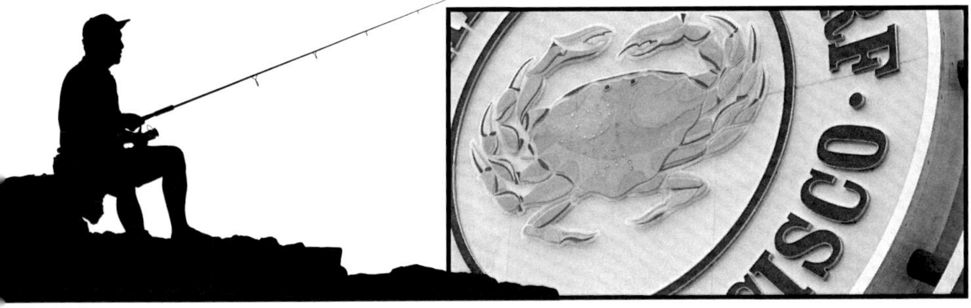

The action here starts in the dark:
To find it, follow sea lions' bark.
Anglers work as barks grow louder,
Stop for a bread bowl of chowder.

15

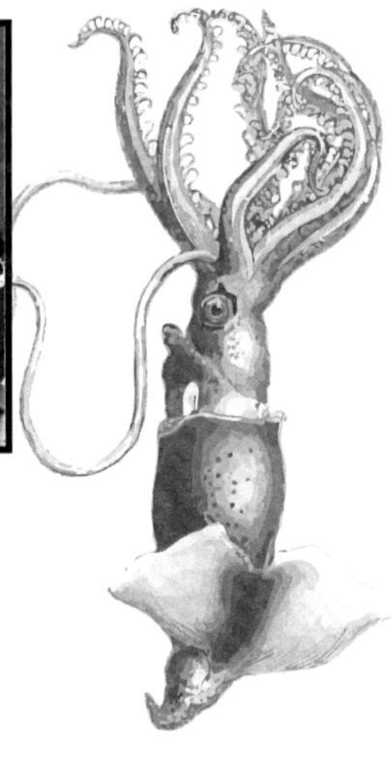

Looking for a salt-watery shocker?
Find creatures here from Davy Jones's Locker.
Quietly they wait for the curious,
But if you pass, they won't be furious.

16

Once this was a spot for ferries;
Now, the list of tenants varies.
Home to a fleet most historic:
For maritime fans, it's euphoric.

17

For seafood, this place is old-school,
When seafaring anglers did rule.
On the pier with views of the bay,
This restaurant's fish dishes do slay.

18

Shining link between sea and sky,
Arc of metal will catch your eye.
Tribute to The True Believer,
Sculptor was a great achiever.

19

Technology that's upwardly mobile,
Assembled by a company global.
Despite ups and downs of which they could boast,
This building served the entire West Coast.

Financial District

This neighborhood (FiDi for short) was underwater when San Francisco was a gold rush town. Buried underneath today's office towers built by old and new titans of industry are more than 100 ships abandoned by those with gold fever.

1

This big work by the Samurai Artist
Is known by a nickname that is smartest.
This particular, glossy piece of art,
To one writer, looked like a weighty heart.

2

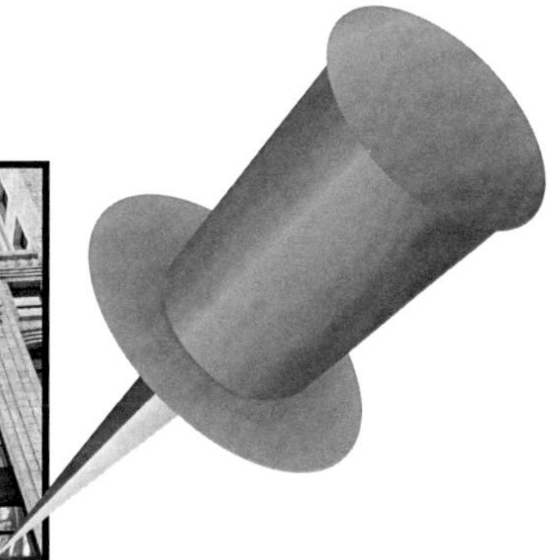

This building decorated with glazed tiles
Is often passed by, but inspires smiles.
It's been compared to a toothpick or pin
Because it is so incredibly thin.

3

Could this be ancient Greece or Rome?
If so, this place might be at home.
Colossal columns on three sides,
In modern SF it resides.

4

This version of an old-world shape
Forever changed local landscape.
Among the city's iconic,
This building's fit is harmonic.

5

Completed by a local starchitect,
With sculpted terra-cotta, it's bedecked.
Its strange shape was dictated by the site,
The building's beauty gives it a bright light.

6

This spot honors certain mail carriers,
Men who were customers of farriers.
These plaques recall an important relay
To deliver the mail without delay.

7

Ghostly figures without a face
Gaze upon the world from this place.
Whether angels or things eerie,
Their perch is surely not dreary.

8

This standing sculpture that's painted in bronze
Among San Francisco's oldest icons.
After the quake, it was a meeting place
For those looking for a familiar face.

9

This celebration of a date
Notes our admission as a state,
From a book angel up in space
To the bronze miner at its base.

10

This narrow place without a door
Marks San Francisco's older shore.
Named for a man who dealt in booze,
Maybe haunted by ghost cow moos.

11

One of the first with a steel frame,
This building survived post-quake's flames.
Heavy footprint forms a letter,
First initial—its begetter.

12

In early morning's golden light,
Montgomery landed near this site.
Once home to an important bank.
This building has historic rank.

13

Once opened as a coffee stand,
Restaurant by immigrants was manned.
Old-school, nostalgic, to be true:
Reservation or face a queue.

14

The city's first glass-curtain-wall tower
Makes one think it's a symbol of power.
It eliminated inside support,
Making cubicles the new office sport.

15

Columns in an orderly row
Support an eagle perch for show.
Former home of a vital bank,
Displayed here its Federal rank.

16

Solution to the city's grid
Made buildings like this a great bid.
Bearing the name of its style,
This one makes Gothic fans smile.

17

At the important gateway to North Beach,
A building standing, nearly white as bleach.
A bank for immigrants from Italy
Still decorates the city prettily.

18

To fans of shipping history,
This building's not a mystery.
Décor the color of the sea
Shows connection to Hawai'i.

19

First founded as a vocational school,
For miners, an educational tool.
With thousands of books, and not one book less,
This building is also well-known for chess.

20

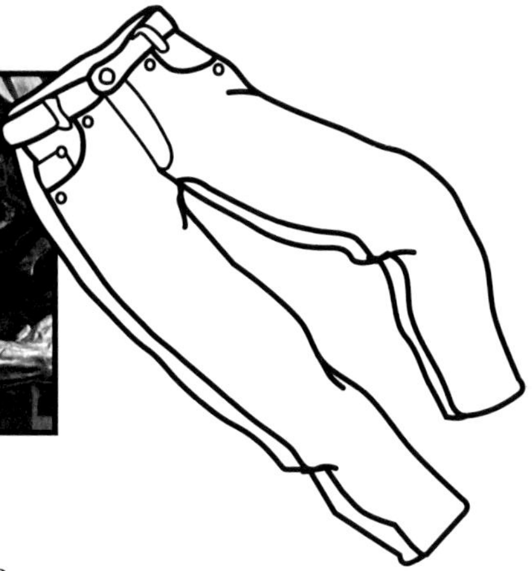

To honor a titan of industry,
This tribute in bronze stands for all to see.
It's not hidden among the landscape plants:
Look for bronze men not wearing any pants.

21

It was once an emperor's residence,
A boardinghouse not fit for presidents.
To slow your frantic San Francisco pace,
Stop and relax in this urban green space.

22

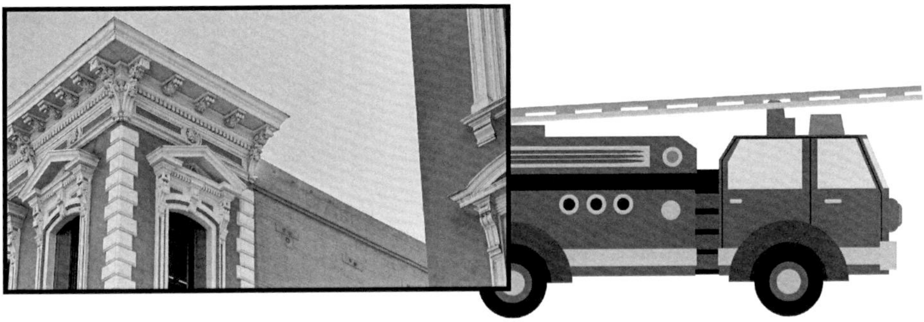

During the great earthquake and fire,
Efforts to save buildings were dire.
This one, spared from becoming ash,
Due to its precious liquid stash.

23

For vice, this neighborhood could boast,
Once known as the Barbary Coast.
Find windows in a half-moon style
For a nightclub that did beguile.

24

It's a delight, designed by an Aussie:
When the water's flowing, it's quite glossy.
Called both a dandelion and peacock's tail,
This public feature never becomes stale.

25

Operating for only 20 years,
Holding gold from California frontiers.
The region's wealth became too large in scope;
The building's function moved so it could cope.

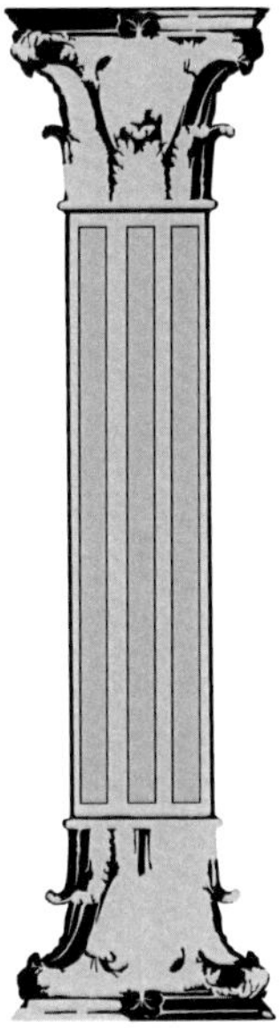

26

A securities market called this home,
Adorned with big columns, and not a dome.
Figures carved in Yosemite granite
From a beautiful spot on the planet.

27

An opulent bonanza inn,
This building was without a twin.
Once, Caruso was sent packing,
Now rebuilt with nothing lacking.

Golden Gate Park

Stretching more than 1,000 acres from the Pacific Ocean to the Haight, Golden Gate Park was built in San Francisco's "Outside Lands" among sand dunes. Today, it's home to some of the city's most-visited attractions and provides a refuge for city dwellers.

1

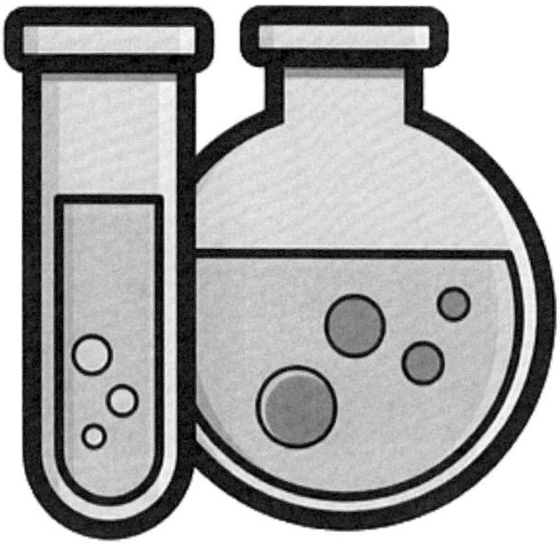

Shrine to the wonder of science,
For humans, has formed alliance.
Contained beneath its earthen roof,
It's building's exhibits hold proof.

2

When you look behind this site's gates,
Oldest of its kind in the states.
Place of Zen, even for rookies,
First to serve certain sweet cookies.

3

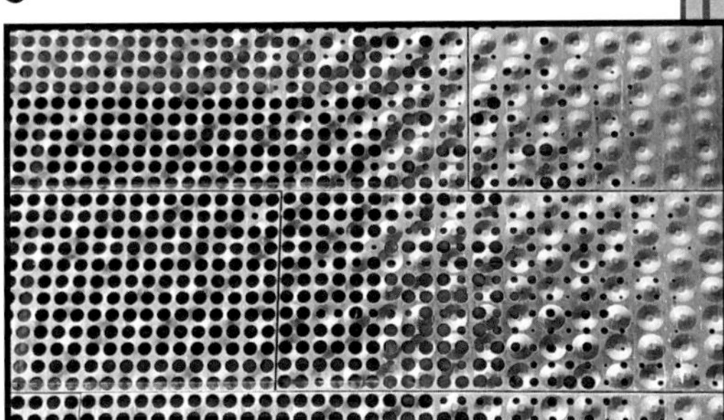

You will go here if you're smart,
To see some American art.
But even more, if you must probe,
There's art here from across the globe.

4

In this graceful spot where plants live,
To pass it by, we don't forgive.
The oldest building in the park,
Victorian style gives it spark.

5

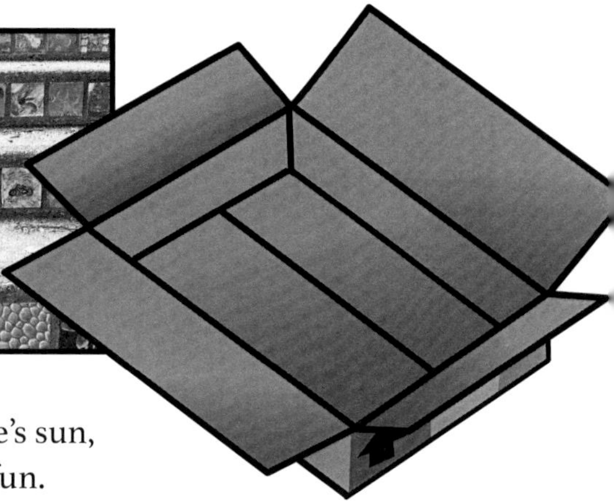

This place, whether or not there's sun,
Is best for some old-fashioned fun.
A longtime fave, the cement slide,
Bring some cardboard to take a ride.

6

Gaze through these tall columns, at last,
What remained when the earthquake passed.
Even though the home is now gone,
City's optimism lives on.

7

If you should knock upon this tiny door,
The occupant may be out for a chore.
If you choose to leave a personal note,
A kind faerie might read the words you wrote.

8

Stones left from an ancient monastery,
Their presence here, is no work of faerie.
They were intended for a grand manor
But were abandoned, without a planner.

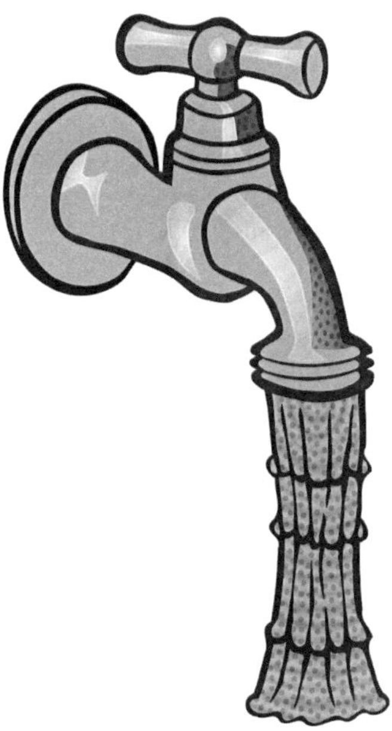

9

Built to pump water for the park,
This tall structure has made its mark.
If one day you see it spinning,
That's a day when you are winning.

10

On a beautiful, sunny day
This is the spot a band would play.
If you're here Sunday afternoon,
Linger a while to hear a tune.

11

Cupids and creatures without regalia
Cavort in a great bronze bacchanalia.
This busy and fantastical design
Tells a fun story about making wine.

12

This Spanish Revival retreat,
For swimmers, was once quite a treat.
Sweeping views of the Pacific
Are actually quite terrific.

13

This natural artwork's biography,
Inspired by tectonic topography.
Is this long, crooked line man-made or not?
You'll soon see, after you find the right spot.

14

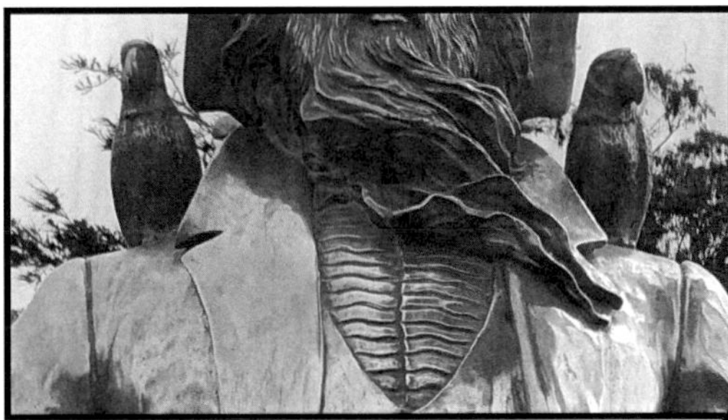

This shiny and modern antihero,
He has far more going on than zero.
With two parrots, two hooks, and two peg-legs,
Leave the rum with this one: he'll drink the dregs.

15

This tribute to a president
Is draped in sadness and lament.
It gave the artist his entrée
To the art world right by the bay.

16

Step gently in this peaceful dell
To remember people who fell.
Space for those affected by AIDS,
A show of love that never fades.

17

Quality time to sit astride
A group of horses for a ride.
Or perhaps you want a dragon?
Go ahead, this is no wagon.

18

Get a close look; it isn't fake,
Saber-toothed tiger with a snake.
A kind gift from a banker's wife,
Appreciation for wildlife.

19

Tucked near a hill along the shore,
This site is not at all a snore.
Gift from sister city Taipei,
A stop here gives a spark to your day.

20

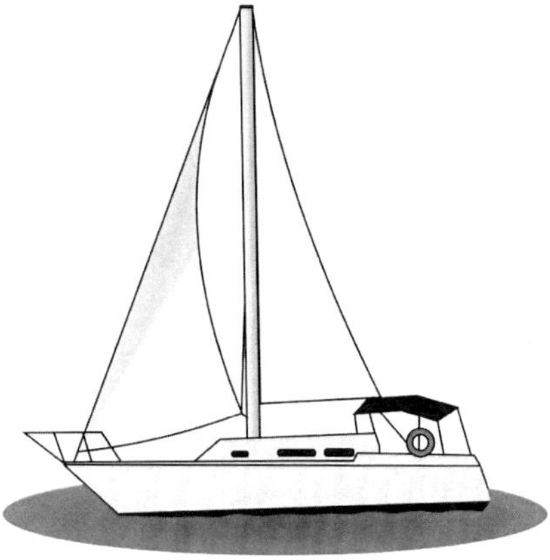

After World War II made its mark,
The first new building in the park.
When you arrive, don't check your notes,
Walk right up to this home for boats.

21

On the sidewalk, will you fiddle?
Will you solve a sphinx's riddle?
This pair is so serene and cool,
Perched next to an enchanted pool.

22

In the park, a quiet jewel
Is right here, this enchanted pool.
Mountain lions listen to boy,
Turtles find the sun to enjoy.

23

This shiny, gilded compass rose,
Even among flowers, it glows.
Movement changes like the weather,
Looking delicate, like a feather.

24

If at first you don't look closely,
Tribute to wine, you'll think: mostly.
Cast your glance a little wider,
You'll see that it's all 'bout cider.

25

Donated by a jewelry store,
This king is far too calm to roar.
Rather, he seems to have some fun
Posing on a rock, in the sun.

26

Tribute to navigators of the sea,
On California's coast, landed these three.
European origin were these guys;
To now say they "discovered" is not wise.

27

A memorial to a Spanish great,
His many works hold literary weight.
Two characters kneel in admiration:
They have never moved from this one station.

28

This tribute to some brave soldiers
Involves a wreath held at shoulders.
The name given by the maker
Makes it sound like he's a baker.

29

Exhibited at the Midwinter Fair,
This bronze sculpture exudes historic flair,
Featuring a weapon in an upswing
For this certain Spartan warrior king.

30

A home and office all in one
For the man who got this park done.
Forty-seven years, if you please,
Credited with 2 million trees.

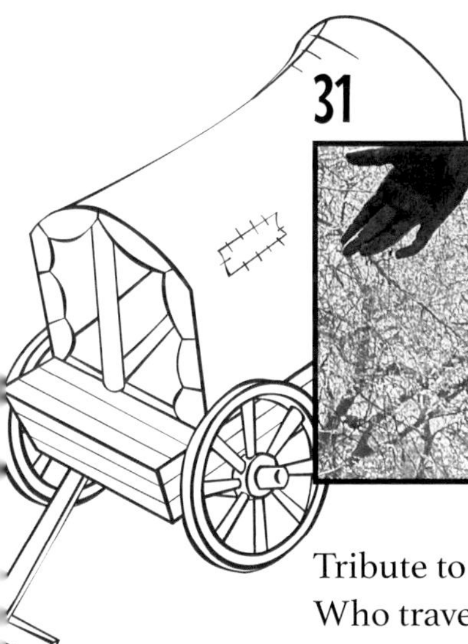

31

Tribute to early pioneers
Who traveled here despite their fears.
Some say this statue is haunted;
Don't wait, if proof is unwanted.

Haight-Ashbury

The rebellious and hippie spirit of '60s counterculture and the Summer of Love still lives on in the Haight. Its café scene, vintage shops, progressive causes, and counterculture nightlife reflect that colorful past.

1

Sparkly high heels and black fishnets
Are among this boutique's assets.
Mostly made to grab attention,
By fans, this site has a mention.

2

Here, upcycling's quirky result
May make you think of the occult.
At your feet, the marble pavers
Are broken pieces from gravers.

3

Fans of game with balls and flippers
Save quarters and ditch their slippers.
Here lives the largest collection,
Simple, but holds great affection.

4

Two-wheel trip from bay to ocean,
At this wiggle, great emotion.
Once was home to a burbling creek,
Along its path, bikers now streak.

5

When this region was still sand dunes,
This Queen Anne house debuted to swoons.
Capped by an open belvedere,
An ideal place to drink a beer.

6

This home may be San Francisco's oldest,
Built when the city was at its goldest.
At that time, this was part of a homestead
It stretched across the multi-acre spread.

7

This fine example of the Queen Anne craft:
Order and ornament, nary a draft.
Its good preservation is quite telling,
It's rare for a single-family dwelling.

8

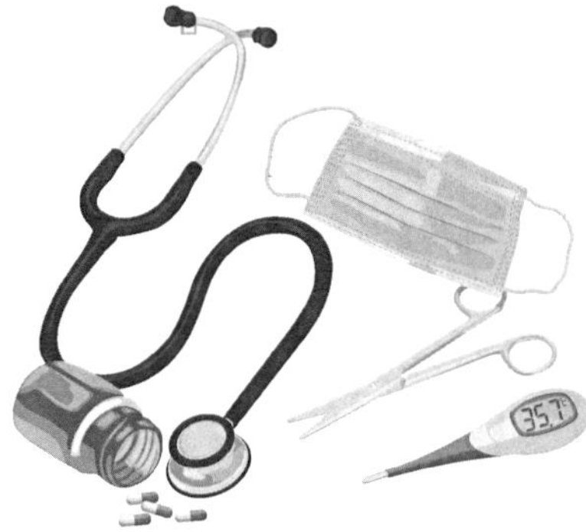

Born in the sweet Summer of Love,
This business's sign includes a dove.
Offering non-judgmental care
For free at the time was quite rare.

9

The home to a local jam band,
This house has historic command,
Making headlines for a drug bust.
People called the dropped charges just.

10

Here's a place you can dive right in,
But here's a tip: They don't serve gin.
Bring some cash and sit right down,
With 40 on tap, it takes the crown.

11

Representing half an acre,
This collection is no faker.
No longer a great place to bowl,
But something better for the soul.

Japantown/ Western Addition

On the southern slopes of Pacific Heights, Nihonmachi (Japantown) began with the settlement of the Japanese community in the mid-19th century. Post-World War II, the Western Addition (especially the Lower Fillmore area) was known as the Harlem of the West for its jazz nightspots.

1

A monument to inspire peace,
As they grow, five stories decrease.
Idea conceived in friendship,
It's a sight that you should not skip.

2

Items inspired by paper folding
Stand in bronze for your beholding.
Planned to resemble flowers,
For the artist, they took hours.

3

Fan of manga and anime?
Follow me, and I'll show the way.
Or perhaps you prefer a book?
You'll leave with something, if you look.

4

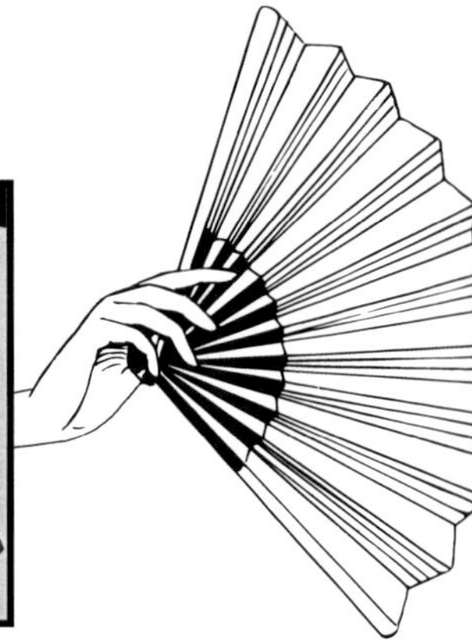

This modern-day *sensu* flares open wide,
A colorful tableau across its side.
Japanese plant motifs show four seasons;
A worthwhile stop here, for many reasons.

5

Family-run store for four generations,
Indoors, this spot has many temptations.
A wealth of home items, including teas,
A treasure of cultural Japanese.

6

History of Japantown on three sides,
Three generations are scholarly guides.
Tribute to Japanese contributions
With hope for amicable solutions.

7

Alternative to public school,
A workaround for a cruel rule.
More than 100 years later,
Language arts are even greater.

8

Women of the Issei generation
Founded the first of these in the nation.
Planned by a California architect,
Programs for women and girls, the subject.

9

This wood-framed building was moved twice,
Oldest of its kind, it's still nice.
Its materials came by ship
Around the Horn: was quite a trip.

10

Row of Victorian sisters
Lures more fans than any misters.
The skyline over a shoulder;
Through the years, they have grown bolder.

11

Once a place known as Majestic,
This venue was not domestic.
Thanks to music businessman Graham,
It became a famed place to jam.

Marina

This picturesque neighborhood overlooking the bay was hammered hard by the 1989 Loma Prieta earthquake, but you'd hardly know by looking at its current, pretty face. Wander along the Marina Green to enjoy the fresh air here, on the northern boundary of San Francisco. It's among the SF neighborhoods with sites that are part of the Golden Gate National Recreation Area (GGNRA).

1

Are these the ruins of a lost city?
From here, the watery view is pretty.
The experience is best at high tide,
Stay quiet: let the bay be your guide.

2

Its life was supposed to be brief,
With concrete, folks sighed with relief.
An elegant landmark, it's true,
Relax on the grass for a view.

3

Building with classic Roman looks,
Inside is filled with tons of books.
One of seven in the city,
Linger, and emerge more witty.

4

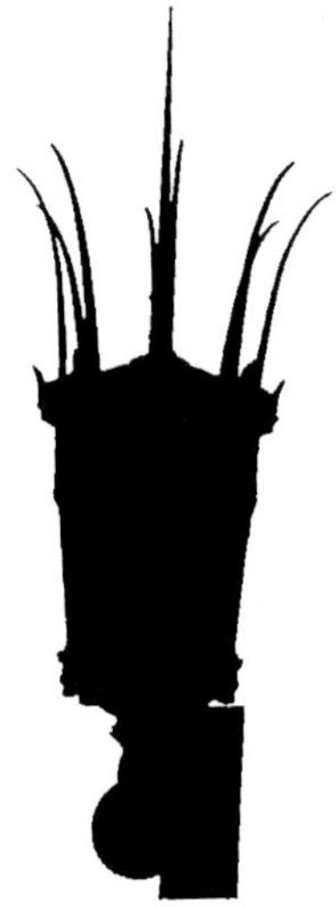

For the Pan-Pacific Exposition,
This building had a specific mission.
Today, its design gains plenty of likes
For fantastic lanterns adorned with spikes.

5

The city planners could not goof
To make firefighting "earthquake-proof."
It's one of two important sites
To get saltwater to great heights.

6

A military post for many years,
Its port sent soldiers off to far frontiers.
Now a part of the GGNRA,
It places culture right beside the bay.

7

This squat structure guards the harbor,
Home to none, even no barber.
A light once used to show the way;
It's been dark for more than a day.

Mission

Once home to Italian and Irish immigrants, the Mission became San Francisco's Latino neighborhood in the late 1960s with new immigrants from Mexico and Central America. Working-class folks and hipsters mix in this district, richly decorated with murals that address political and social justice issues.

1

When you need something sweet and cool,
Find this old-school Mission jewel.
If there's a line, you should brave it,
This rich ice cream, you will crave it.

2

When other forms of fun you've tried,
Stop by this place to take a ride.
A smart tip not to be ignored:
Be sure to bring your own cardboard.

3

If for pirates ye be searchin',
Drop right in; don't be an urchin.
Among this stop's special features:
Pirate shop for woodland creatures.

4

The oldest structure is antique,
Nickname comes from a nearby creek.
With 20 sisters in the state,
This is the one that's remained great.

____

____

5

For some, artwork can be quite small;
To others, canvas is a wall.
This block packs colors together
To enjoy in any weather.

____

____

6

The water sources were nearly zero,
But the Great Fire produced this small hero.
It saved the Mission, as the story's told,
That's why, in honor, it's been painted gold.

7

Inspired by a place called Balmy,
Artists have not tried to draw me.
Better yet, the bright collection
Shows the city's true complexion.

8

Italian Renaissance for looks,
But inside, it's brimming with books.
After the big earthquake came forth,
The fire stopped four blocks north.

9

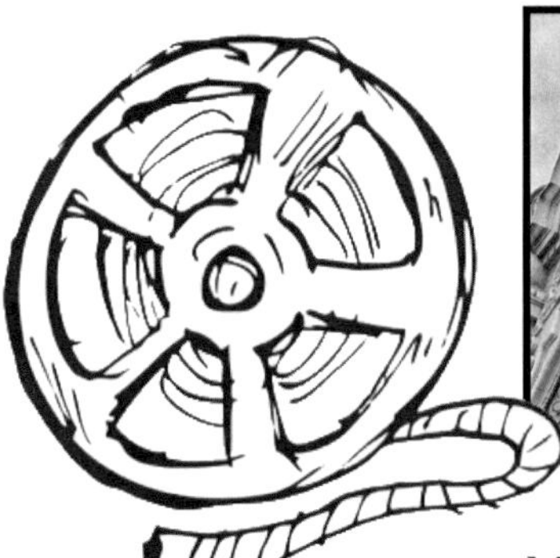

Mexican Baroque façade is what's left;
Without all the rest, film fans are bereft.
Those people who loved it called it The Cap,
Once second-largest on the city map.

10

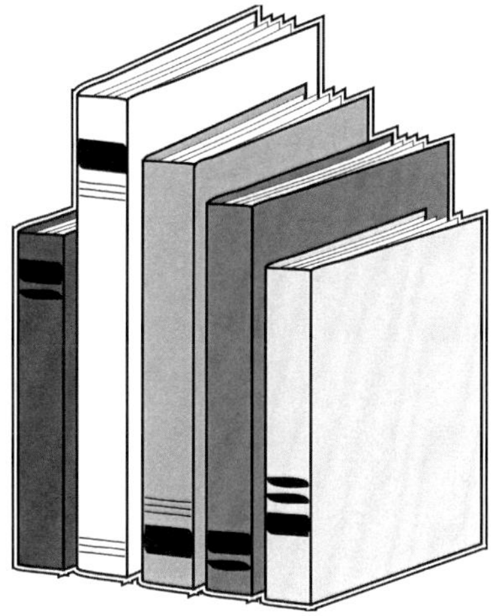

Turn down the corner if you must,
A page, not a canine adjust.
I must confess to have perused
Some volumes previously used.

11

Built as a gathering place for girls,
Whether or not they could wear pearls.
Now, serves broader community,
Goal of neighborhood unity.

12

With thick, brick walls like a castle,
Approval here wasn't facile.
Built to store weapons securely,
It's had other uses, surely.

13

Seventy-foot sign says it's new,
With its first reuse, that was true.
Saved from death, it then added space,
Brief escape from the rat race.

14

This building predates the earthquake,
It served those who needed a break.
Today, continues its labors
To take care of all its neighbors.

15

Former governor's ancestor,
An original investor.
From vaudeville to film to burlesque,
In age, it remains statuesque.

16

This building's colorful exterior,
Among others, is far superior.
Marking some great women's contributions,
While inside, they still work on solutions.

17

The pastries here are sweet and fine,
But if you want one, get in line.
The time will pass, out in the sun,
Then you may taste a morning bun.

18

Mission burritos, you have guessed,
Few people agree which is best.
The ones served here are more than nice,
More room for meat when there's no rice.

19

Murals, the Mission has a lot,
As you wander, many you'll spot.
Don't pass this alley too quickly:
It's here where paint is spread thickly.

20

A pioneer of Latin rock
In black and white on this street block.
Four blocks from where he went to school,
Long before he was known as cool.

21

This center is quite emphatic:
Culture isn't something static.
Focused on living tradition
Of the people of the Mission.

22

You may think it is just a dive,
That's before you've seen events live.
The inclusive space gets high praise,
Notably on Salsa Sundays.

23

Known for bloody Marys and beers,
A spot around for many years.
The garden is the place to be,
Even when Karl the fog won't flee.

Nob Hill

Named for the "nabobs" who built their hilltop estates here (Charles Crocker, Leland Stanford, Mark Hopkins, and Collis P. Huntington), Snob Hill became Nob Hill over time. While the 1906 earthquake and fire destroyed many of those palatial mansions, there's still plenty remaining to see.

1

Quote: "Weaving spiders come not here,"
Says more than a love for Shakespeare.
Exclusive club for only dudes,
Leave business outside, note alludes.

2

If in search of Tuscan cuisine,
Roll on in to this old-school scene.
Favorite neighborhood spot for years,
Pasta dishes bring loyal cheers.

3

Take a breath and shed all that stress,
Walking this line needs no finesse.
Meditation is easy here,
In little time, your mind is clear.

4

Built over years, for quite a price,
Guarded by gates of paradise.
When opened, 5,000 did bring,
Including Martin Luther King.

5

The original rests in Rome,
Copy purchased for Crocker's home.
Look carefully for its namesake,
Things that thieves have been known to take.

6

Group of three dancing together,
Draped in ribbon, not a feather.
Their youthful joy is all abud,
This bronze piece, gifted from a Flood.

7

If you love saltiness of brine,
Have some patience and wait in line.
Pick your favorite dish to savor
Just-caught-from-the-ocean flavor.

8

The 19th-century transportation
Is celebrated at this location.
Much more than just a look into the past:
History has found a fun way to last.

9

First of international brand
Atop a hill, forever grand.
A place of firsts, as it turns out,
Beloved by all, without a doubt.

10

Well-known for luxury and style,
You'd be lucky to stay a while.
Former insurance co., doubly,
Now a place to drink some bubbly.

11

Named after a railroad founder,
Elegance you may encounter.
For soldiers during World War II,
Top was best to enjoy the view.

12

If looking for a taste of France,
Go right here, if you have the chance.
Relax, peruse the list of wine,
A cool lounge vibe makes you feel fine.

13

Right where the cable car lines cross,
A mansion for a railroad boss.
All that remains is fence and wall,
Replaced by different building's sprawl.

14

I promise this is not a drill:
A wild animal prowls Nob Hill.
Different ursine than with honey,
Serious and not as funny.

15

This bronze of a long-beloved crooner,
Unveiled at 90, not a day sooner.
Not known for rap music or for disco,
He sang about love for San Francisco.

16

White and curvy like wedding cake,
If you bite it, your tooth will ache.
Influenced by Beaux-Arts décor,
Gorgeous building is not a bore.

17

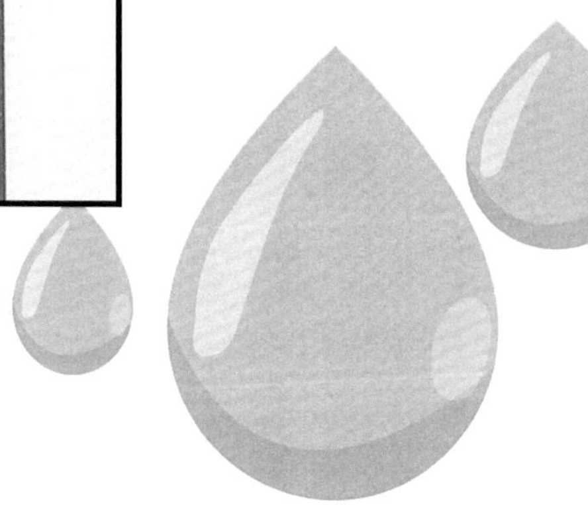

A lesson learned from the earthquake:
Fire can often follow the shake.
This spot holds a lot of water,
Stops a spark from getting hotter.

18

Townhouse for a silver tycoon
(After he started a saloon).
With brownstone shipped around the Cape,
The earthquake didn't change its shape.

19

Neo-Georgian home, quite petite,
Stands out from others on the street.
Originally a coachman's house,
Now dedicated to a spouse.

North Beach/ Telegraph Hill

At the time of the gold rush, North Beach was really a beach, and the neighborhood was once almost exclusively Italian American. From then, through the Barbary Coast and beatnik eras, North Beach and Telegraph Hill have retained their heart and soul from the old days.

1

Today, while looking through the stacks,
It all started with paperbacks.
Alternative culture landmark,
In the '50s, it lit a spark.

2

It first appeared in a jungle village,
But was destroyed after Army pillage.
This copy is a great show of support
For a struggle that's anything but short.

3

World geography you may know,
But here, this is no volcano.
Pilgrims know throughout the nation,
Spot for the Beat Generation.

4

Built on the site of a key bank
After Fugazi, to be frank.
A woman, the building's donor,
Mark of an empowered owner.

5

Where two neighborhoods meet along your walk,
Look up for quite a different kind of flock.
Beneath your feet, a collection of words
From a cultured group of non-feathered birds.

6

While this business is not antique,
The site's history is unique.
In early days, the room did swell
With some mafia clientele.

7

People with quite a bit of clout
Frequented this North Beach hangout.
Late-night home to Beats and actors,
Well-beloved, with few detractors.

8

A longtime local surely knows
This place of booze and curios.
Blend of counterculture, drinking
Fits perfectly here, I'm thinking.

9

It's far, far north of Hollywood,
But in film, it's considered good.
Much beloved by Dirty Harry,
Where Marilyn did not marry.

10

Tribute to a founding father,
Many pass without a bother.
Tucked inside, a time capsule fine,
Unearth it in ’79.

11

Named for a favorite baseball son,
Only goal here is to have fun.
Stop on by for a pickup game
Or play bocce for local fame.

12

This building is known by some different names,
Its beauty admired in all the claims.
The distinctive look is due to copper,
The view from the street is a showstopper.

13

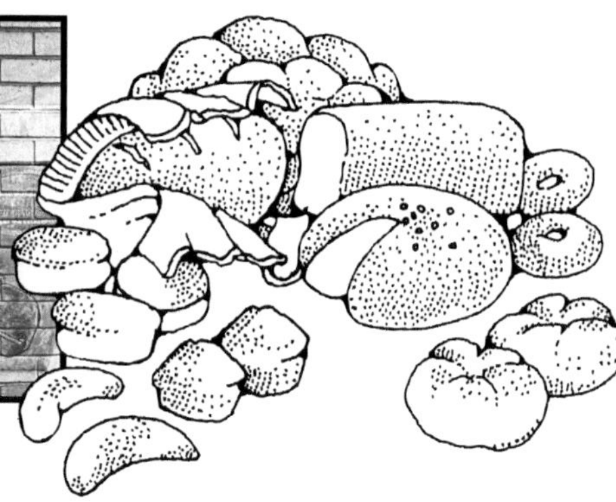

If you are looking for a tasty treat,
It is agreed that this spot can't be beat.
If I had more money, I'd have bought ya
A bag full of delicious focaccia.

14

The first for espresso on the West Coast,
It's known far and wide for delicious roast.
A meeting place for authors and artists,
Regular customers are the smartest.

15

If you worship at the sandwich altar,
Head right to this place: don't even falter.
Open for longer than 100 years,
Their reviews always amount to loud cheers.

16

Named after its owner and not the bread,
Known for glamour and artists who shred.
For a good time, whether wild or saner,
Find a date with a great entertainer.

17

Built with money from socialite Lillie,
This sleek memorial is not silly.
Dedicated to the firefighters,
It has inspired more than just writers.

18

Built by an immigrant, this quirky home
Stands tall and thin, and crowned with a blue dome.
It's hard to spy, even from Gogna's gate,
The myths behind it are up for debate.

19

Between the waterfront and Coit Tower,
This route climbs up high, through leaf and flower.
The challenging status has its merit,
Try your best to spy a local parrot.

Pacific Heights

San Francisco's most pricey and dramatic real estate is in this tony neighborhood, where folks with old and new money rub elbows. From grand Victorians to quaint Queen Annes, impressive homes with spectacular views are plentiful.

1

Is it complete, or only half?
Perhaps an architect's big gaffe.
Built as mirror of another
For a sister, not a brother.

2

If you're a Victorian fan,
You'll appreciate this Queen Anne.
The merchant for whom it was made
Immigrated to find his trade.

3

Painted in gold for all to see,
This sculpture in a place that's key:
Migrants have made this city great
For stellar views, relax and wait.

4

What to do when you have money to blow?
You find a prime lot and build a chateau.
With a sugar fortune, this man did pay
For a large home with sweet views of the bay.

____

____

5

Built for a Valparaíso bride,
She moved here when her husband died.
Its style has been called eclectic,
Its reported ghosts are hectic.

____

____

6

This nice building's architectural plan
Is, unusually, purely a Queen Anne.
More hybrid and decorative styles appear
On some other Victorian homes here.

7

This architect's palatial house,
Designed for himself and his spouse.
In front, it looks two stories high,
The rear's taller, when you walk by.

8

Giant mansion of clinker brick
May make East Coasters feel homesick.
Its owner had a fortune fine
At 17, from a gold mine.

9

This brick home was a wedding gift,
Its style, restrained, is quite a shift.
Husband was a master of tea,
A company with letters three.

10

It's number six in the public system,
Long filled with things that can impart wisdom.
Italian-Renaissance in its design,
For those seeking knowledge, it's a lifeline.

11

Part of an extensive estate,
This house was built Italianate.
An old one in this neighborhood,
Its blacksmith owner thought it good.

12

This home of a mining mogul,
From the street, it's hard to ogle.
Now home to a ghost, some may fear,
But no one with that name lived here.

13

Moved from its original site,
Former doctors' home's a delight.
Don't believe me and need some proof?
Look at the pretty mansard roof.

14

Called a "balustrade-y affair,"
This mansion was built with great care.
Oval windows, pointy surrounds,
Among the features of these grounds.

15

This building, once a firehouse,
Handsome, yet simple as a mouse.
Try to spy the single tower,
Hoses dried after a shower.

16

One of the first homes made of stone,
Classy residence was well-known.
Made for an iron and steel man
In this home, had a brief lifespan.

17

Former home of a temple school,
To bookmakers, became a jewel.
Fine books were made at this address,
Copper mansard roof to impress.

18

A building in Medieval style
Housed the Knights Templar for a while.
Masonic temple to a church,
Those who know the right research.

19

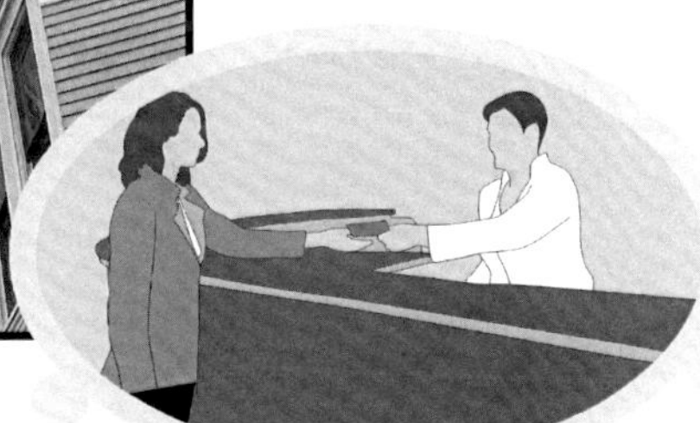

This nearly unchanged, pre-fire home,
Gilt and dignified, like a poem.
Desire luxury? You may stay
As many days as you can pay.

20

A wedding present for a son
Of wood and stucco, not outdone.
Building showed its variety
For the historic society.

21

"Boston House" from around the Horn,
Simple in style since it was born.
Its owner helped acquire park land,
At the time, made from dunes of sand.

22

Designed by famous architects,
Beautiful Arts and Crafts effects.
Sheltered by a heavy tile roof,
The sanctuary is rainproof.

23

Not the congregation's first home,
Building is noted for its dome.
Surviving both fire and earthquake,
Its masonry proved hard to break.

24

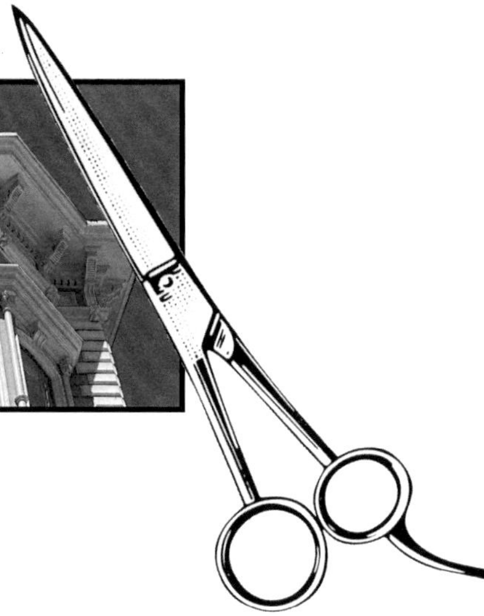

Among our Victorian pearls,
This beauty was a home for girls.
Named for Black woman millionaire,
Who made her fortune in hair care.

25

It's rumored that ghosts roam and moan
In this mansion made of sandstone.
After first owners' lives were spent,
Sold to the Nazi government.

26

This pretty pair of Queen Anne homes
Are known for more than just their domes.
Look below, not for a feather,
Bands that look like ostrich leather.

27

Workplace of a famous nanny
In film, man dressed as a granny.
This turreted Victorian,
Known to movie historian.

Presidio

For more than 200 years, the Presidio served as an army post, under the flags of three nations: Spain, Mexico, and the United States. It's now a thriving park in the city's northwestern corner and part of the Golden Gate National Recreation Area.

1

More than 1 mile across its span,
Structure was a challenge to plan.
If you require a bigger clue,
International Orange: hue.

2

Those who like walking along Lover's Lane
Miss this one item, time and time again.
But next time, look deeper yet, if you could,
A flowing line of eucalyptus wood.

3

One of many in the Presidio,
This military site is one to know.
While you're visiting, and before you're done,
Look around for the disappearing gun.

4

When you're wandering through Fort Point,
Find this spot at a bridge viewpoint.
Made for runners who tap the fence,
Enthusiasm to dispense.

5

Made up of 35 large cypress trees,
This grand sculpture may bring you to your knees.
Nature is known to transform over time:
Thus, this site will always be in its prime.

6

Do or do not; there is no try:
Find a likeness of this old guy.
Now, be calmed by his quiet gaze.
Benefit you will, all your days.

7

Whether you exit or enter,
By car, you'd go through the center.
These dear portals made of sandstone,
On the east side, they are well-known.

8

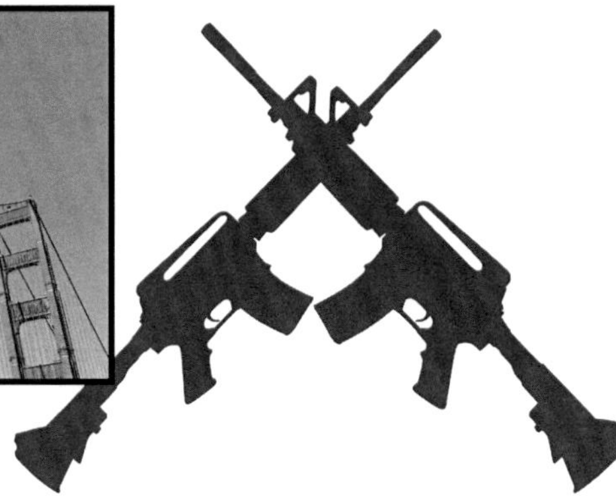

A sturdy guard of the narrows
Protect from cannons, not arrows.
Although it never saw battle,
With guns plenty, it did rattle.

9

When you are a little chilly,
Whether dressed plain or quite frilly,
Duck inside this historic space.
Get hot chocolate to warm your face.

10

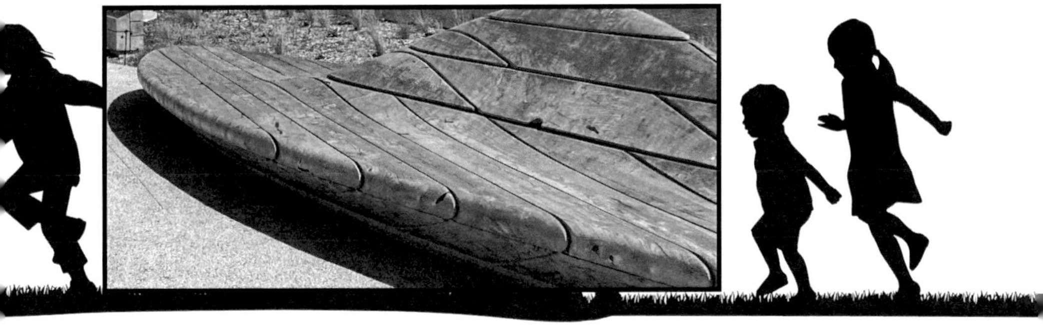

Built on top of parkway tunnels,
This is where outdoor joy funnels.
Even on a gray, foggy day,
This is the place kids want to play.

11

A former home to Army troops,
Buildings know how to handle groups.
Beautiful view, before you spread,
This quiet place to rest your head.

Richmond/ Lincoln Park

Along San Francisco's wild western shoreline, the Richmond district shares space with Lands End and Lincoln Park and has some of the best Golden Gate views. Like the Sunset district, the Richmond was once covered in sand dunes and fog—well, it still has the fog.

1

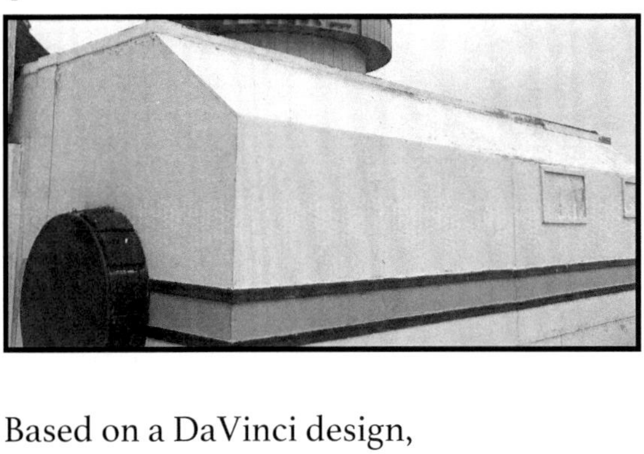

Based on a DaVinci design,
For photo fans, it is a shrine.
With a 360-degree view,
Historic spots like this are few.

2

For a millionaire with a dream,
The massive glass building did gleam.
A splendid engineering feat,
Now, only pieces of concrete.

3

Once made for the city's coastal defense,
The construction cost more than a few cents.
Its very important guns are now gone,
Although its Army history lives on.

4

Long depicting contemplation,
Bronze form with rock as its station.
From days to nights, sunshine to fog,
A statue as still as a log.

5

Home for local and global art,
Park surroundings set it apart.
First opened on Armistice Day,
It's become a good place to stray.

6

Excellent place, without a doubt,
This building where you can look out.
Tucked at an end point of the land,
Far above the ocean and sand.

7

A memorial to a valiant crew
Who all fought on this ship in World War II.
Many people may walk past this locale,
A historic link to Guadalcanal.

8

A sculpture by a native son
Was controversial on day one.
Big and strong in a hue that's bright,
Standing tall on a tilt that's slight.

9

This memorial to millions,
Not soldiers, but dead civilians.
Figures are painted in stark white,
A history revealed by light.

10

When built, its backyard was just sand,
Former home of a slick rock band.
Party house painted black and gold,
White again when the building sold.

11

Once home to a youth organization
With membership from across the nation.
Known for its Bay Area Craftsman style,
Continues to serve children with a smile.

12

The first here with this man's money,
Filled with books, some of them funny.
Of the original seven,
All are bibliophile heaven.

13

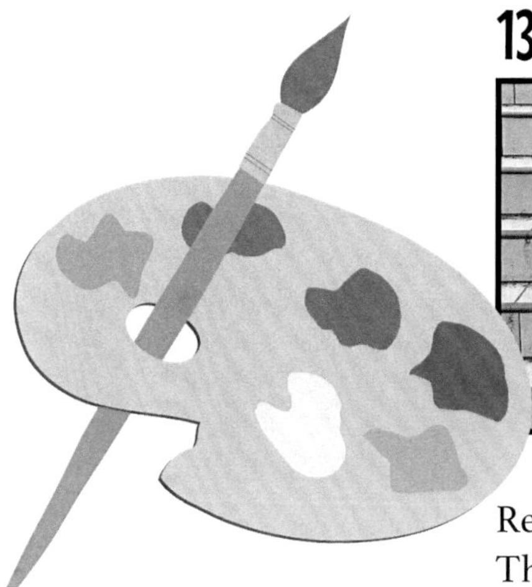

Relax and hear a gentle hush,
This is far from a place to rush.
With bright colors to pierce the gray,
Step down to enjoy the display.

14

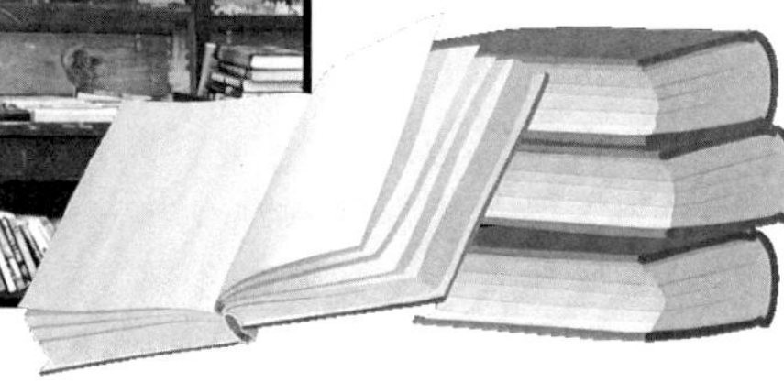

When from your work you have been freed,
Visit this spot for those who read.
Beloved by its fans far and wide,
Let the book people be your guide.

15

Founded by patriarch Tomás,
Family business you'll come across.
I'll run faster than a cheetah
For their famous margarita.

Russian Hill

One of the oldest neighborhoods in San Francisco, Russian Hill is named for the Russian gravestones found at the top of the hill by people who came during the gold rush. With some of the city's steepest streets, it also has some of the best bay views.

1

This example of Moorish Revival
Wowed visitors upon their arrival.
Once used for a cinematic escape,
Now it is used for getting into shape.

2

Built to stand atop Russian Hill
For fire reasons, not a drill.
Made in Craftsman and Tudor style,
Getting engines here took a while.

3

One of only three left in the city,
It is quite rare, and it's also pretty.
It was a national fad in its day
For each room to have its own sunlight ray.

4

From valley farms to nearby pier,
Fruit and veg were delivered here.
First a cannery, then much more,
This building with its brick décor.

5

It's one of the city's oldest buildings;
Over the years, it has seen many things.
From chocolate treats to soldiers' uniforms,
Representing goods in their many forms.

6

This small enclave in Russian Hill
Has beautiful views that will thrill.
In tales of the city, this place
Has a very familiar face.

7

Once a school for people practicing art,
This place gave budding artists a big start.
Its fertile spirit of innovation
Inspired many across the nation.

8

The way here may be very steep,
You're rewarded with views that sweep.
This site perfect for a poet,
It's claimed for one, don't you know it.

9

In order to find this striped dude,
Helps to be in a playful mood.
Not the man himself, just the same
Famous stripes, and also his name.

10

This celebration of abundant curves
Is what you'll see through several gentle swerves.
It's not the same as the yellow brick road,
The color is red, though traffic is slowed.

11

No longer a bathhouse for troops,
Building lures sea-curious groups.
Its contents are no mystery,
Feature seafaring history.

12

This spot at the end of the line
Helps a vehicle realign.
Before you go the other way,
The car must turn, without delay.

13

When a cup of coffee you wish,
Stop by here, but make it Irish.
A fun bar study: one to gloat,
Long hours were spent to make cream float.

14

Is this scene from beneath the sea?
T'was the artist's priority.
Working in bronze, when she was done,
It is enjoyed by everyone.

15

With chocolate, this location grew
Delighting more than just a few.
Project for adaptive reuse
For the future lit quite a fuse.

SoMa/South Beach

The large swath of blocks that stretch from east to west beneath Market Street is the SoMa (South of Market) and South Beach neighborhood. The sunny district, once an industrial center, is now home to rich cultural museums, hotels, restaurants, and a bayside ballpark.

1

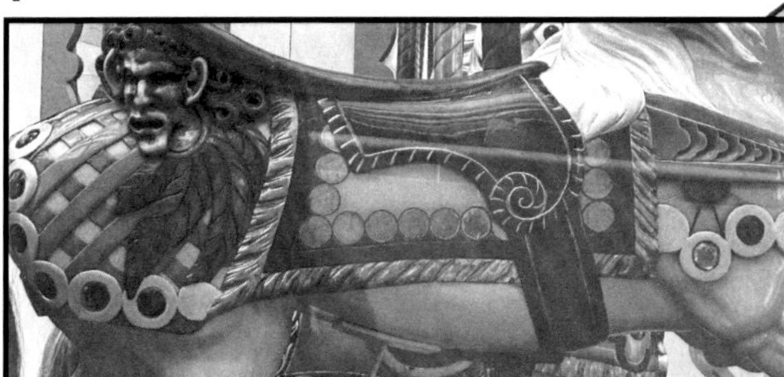

The earthquake and fire delayed its placement,
But this Looff didn't stay in the basement.
Its animals twirl around in a ring,
Thanks to a very thoughtful man named King.

2

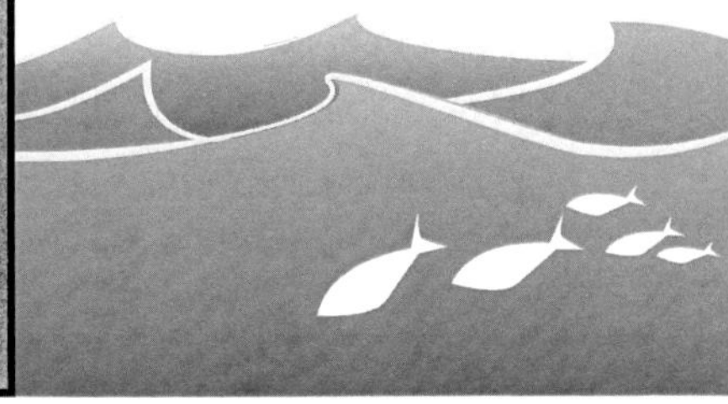

Follow the coastline in this spot,
You think it's one thing, but it's not.
Shoreline boundary has shifted,
With fill, land it has been gifted.

3

Could a merman catch a baseball?
With a glove and without one fall.
If gods and goddesses could play,
They'd pick the City by the Bay.

4

Things are hard to miss when they're red,
It's as if there's a light ahead.
This giant work that's kinetic
Adds to the city's aesthetic.

5

Does god Eros have a home port?
This fair city is just the sort.
Perhaps his tools may give a clue,
Stand back to get a complete view.

6

Say, hey, have you seen this great superstar?
A giant swing and eyes gazing afar.
A fine meeting place for many a fan,
It's right here, in the shadow of the man.

7

This, inspired by a great opera star
Who survived the earthquake without a scar.
This canopy of grand and baby grand,
It's up above the sidewalk where you stand.

8

This building that includes some Irish stone,
Among modern neighbors, it stands alone.
Its Gothic Revival architecture
Could fill many a professor's lecture.

9

Look for the floral letter A,
And your solution's on the way.
Built in a French commercial style,
This building's been around awhile.

10

A collection of fanciful creatures
Are the highlight of the entrance features.
Look above for the crest with a letter
In honor of this wealthy go-getter.

11

This building with a modern collection
Has a contemporary direction.
Central cylinder is the biggest clue
Of the great art inside, awaiting you.

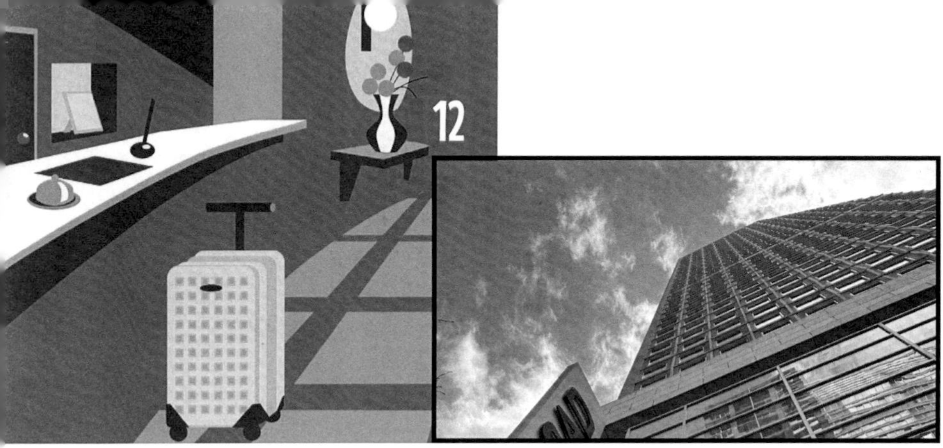

12

In a SoMa hotel's ground floor,
A wonderful place to explore.
Black cultural celebration
In this site of inspiration.

13

This big place of major league fame
Now wears its fourth official name.
Home to giants, more than twenty,
It's on TV screens aplenty.

14

If you like quiet above all,
Search out this city waterfall.
Memorial inspiration,
Loved by those throughout the nation.

15

When through the city you may dash,
Pause right here for a pleasing splash.
No, of swimming I'm not speaking,
Sound of water gently streaking.

16

The beautiful skill of paper folding
In stainless steel is what you're beholding.
Move over a little: but just a smidge,
To make it a big frame for the Bay Bridge.

17

San Francisco's maritime history
Includes this place: it is no mystery.
An example of cooperation
Between the land and sea at this station.

18

State's wealth of silver and gold
Was too much for one place to hold.
National importance for years,
This "old" place of the new frontiers.

19

Streamline moderne, a new era,
Commute traffic and mail to "Dear Sarah."
With animals like dolphins and eagle
On this building, nothing is less regal.

20

Steel-framed, and clad in Sierra granite,
A building prettier, few could plan it.
It is a circuit home for appeals,
Helps to uphold the country's ideals.

21

Combine a historic power station
With blue steel in this exact location.
The Hebrew word for "life" is in its shape,
Part of a contemporary landscape.

22

This center for art and progress,
A place to embrace change, no less.
Exploring doesn't prohibit
Search for a favorite exhibit.

23

In days of the Barbary Coast,
Businesses like saloons thrived most.
Once used for seasonal workers,
Now bar and stage for non-lurkers.

24

The tide swings high; the tide swings low,
Where it is now, these poles will show.
A little bit of science fun
While you're out for a walk or run.

25

Rail transit, whether fast or slow,
Vintage cars are the way to go.
Stop here to learn their history,
Donations help, but enter free.

26

This working-class institution,
A tasty and cheap solution.
Named for some seafaring brothers,
It's now beloved by others.

27

The turning point of a maritime strike,
Emotion caused violence to spike.
Memorial to Bloody Thursday dead,
Their work for the labor movement to spread.

Sunset

The Sunset's realm runs along the southern edge of Golden Gate Park and beyond to San Francisco's western coastline. Much of this district was built atop the sand dunes that covered western San Francisco into the 19th century.

1

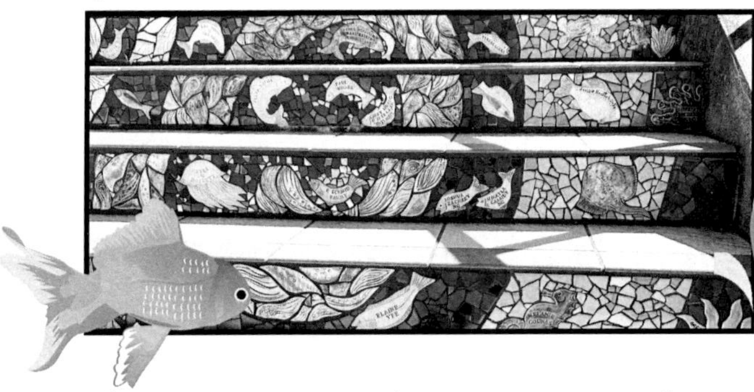

The sea gives way to the stars, moon, and sun
In this sweet place, where fantasy is fun.
Climb from low to high, or from high to low,
Take your time to enjoy them and go slow.

2

A garden always has some hidden things:
Tiny flowers, snails, mushrooms, insect wings.
Walk along this uphill path to find some:
The walk here will keep you from feeling glum.

3

This place to connect with wildlife,
Good spot to escape daily strife.
Not just a place for distraction,
Inspires conservation action.

4

Whether for breakfast or a post-beach lunch,
A meal at this spot packs a tasty punch.
Caffeine lovers do enjoy the java:
Locally roasted; cooler than lava.

5

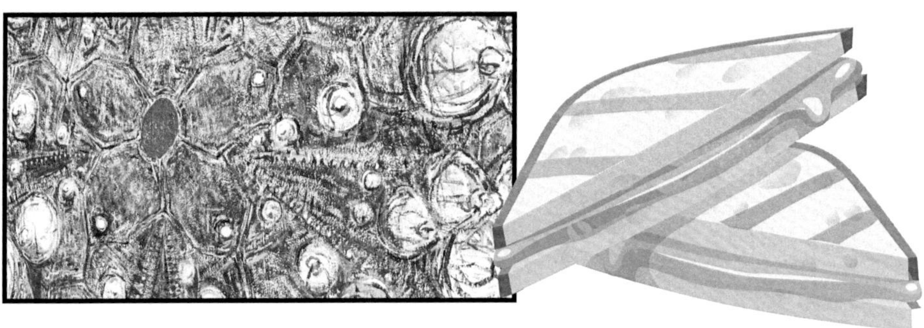

Covered in driftwood, like the beach,
A few blocks away, within reach.
Finding great food here is a breeze;
If you're like me, get the grilled cheese.

6

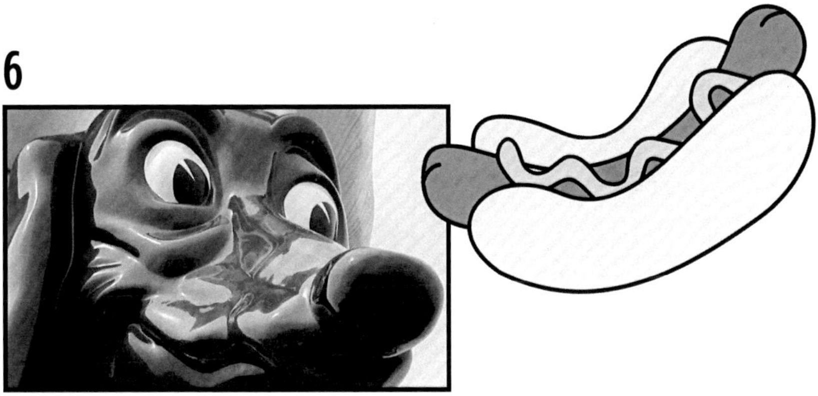

This greatly beloved local chain,
No more permanent signs remain.
Its fast-food menu, doggone fine,
Advertised by a red canine.

7

After the great fire and earthquake,
Thousands of these, did SF make.
Tiny houses for refugees,
To give shelter from the sea breeze.

8

Back when this place was well-known as Carville,
Covered in shingles, this building was chill.
Artists and health seekers liked to live there,
Otherwise, year-round renters were quite rare.